Susan Sontag

ALICE IN BED

Alice in Bed is a free dramatic fantasy based on a real person, Alice James (1848–92), the brilliant sister of William and Henry James. The waters of depression closed over Alice James when she was nineteen: she tried to summon the courage to commit suicide, she suffered from a variety of vague and debilitating ailments, she went abroad, she stayed in bed, she kept a diary, and she died . . . at forty-four.

In Susan Sontag's play, Alice James merges imaginatively with the other great Alice of her period, the heroine of Lewis Carroll's *Alice in Wonderland*. A tea party is convened where Alice is counseled by Emily Dickinson and Margaret Fuller and by two exemplary angry women from the nineteenth-century stage: Myrtha, the Queen of the Wilis, from *Giselle*; and (from Wagner's *Parsifal*) Kundry, the guilt-ridden woman who wants to sleep.

Alice in Bed is a play about the anguish and grief and rage of women, and finally, about the imagination, its triumphs and its limitations. It is a powerful and memorable addition to Susan Sontag's multifaceted achievement as a writer.

Susan Sontag's *The Volcano Lover* was a runaway bestseller in 1992. She lives in New York, where she is at work on another novel.

PAPERBACK:
0-374-52385-1 .
HARDCOVER:
0-374-10273-2

By Susan Sontag

Fiction

THE BENEFACTOR

DEATH KIT

I, ETCETERA

THE WAY WE LIVE NOW

THE VOLCANO LOVER

Essays

AGAINST INTERPRETATION

STYLES OF RADICAL WILL

ON PHOTOGRAPHY

ILLNESS AS METAPHOR

UNDER THE SIGN OF SATURN

AIDS AND ITS METAPHORS

Filmscripts

DUET FOR CANNIBALS

BROTHER CARL

Play

ALICE IN BED

A SUSAN SONTAG READER

ALICE IN BED

ALICE IN BED

A PLAY IN

EIGHT SCENES

BY SUSAN SONTAG

FARRAR·STRAUS·GIROUX

NEW YORK

Designed by Cynthia Krupat
First edition, 1993

CIP data TK

MANUFACTURED BY :
THE COUNTRY PRESS INC.
MIDDLEBOROUGH, MA

ALICE IN BED

ALICE JAMES
NURSE
YOUNG MAN

Visions of family
FATHER
HENRY ("HARRY"), *her brother*
MOTHER

At the tea party
MARGARET FULLER
EMILY DICKINSON
MYRTHA, *Queen of the Wilis (from* Giselle)
KUNDRY *(from* Parsifal)

Mattress team
M I *(man)*
M II *(woman)*

———

TIME: *1890*
PLACE: London
    *(Scene 3 is a flashback or memory, and takes place two
    decades earlier in Cambridge, Massachusetts)*

Roles that could be doubled:
FATHER *(who might be played by a woman) and* MARGARET
EMILY *and* M II
NURSE *and* KUNDRY
MOTHER *and* MYRTHA
YOUNG MAN *and* M I

SCENE 1

Blackout (ALICE's bedroom)

NURSE's Voice
Of course you can get up.

ALICE's Voice
I can't.

NURSE
Won't.

ALICE
Can't

NURSE
Won't.

ALICE
Can't. Oh. All right.

NURSE
Want to. Want to get up.

ALICE
First turn on the light.

SCENE 2

ALICE's *bedroom. Victorian, overfurnished. French doors in the rear. Chaise longue, piano.* ALICE—*around forty, long hair, childlike—in a large brass bed, under a stack (ten?) of thin mattresses; her head, shoulders, and arms are free.* NURSE, *who is very tall and wears a uniform of striped mattress ticking, is perched cross-legged on top.*

NURSE
Are you going to get up. It's only a question of willpower.

ALICE
I think it's time for my injection.

NURSE
Don't change the subject.

ALICE
I'm not. My legs don't work.

NURSE
I know the time. He's coming at four. You like to please him. He'd be so happy to see you sitting up, in a chair.

ALICE
I wonder. I think he likes to see me in bed.

/

NURSE
Whatever for.

(She jumps or climbs down)

ALICE
That way he knows where I am. I'm in my place.

NURSE
They visit. Your brother. Your friends.

ALICE
Friends who are curious. They want to see if I'm still alive. They're waiting. I'm disappointing them.

NURSE
Wouldn't you care to visit them, lazybones. Aren't you in the least bit curious. Haven't you had enough of this room.

ALICE
Go out. See, as they say, the world.

NURSE
Yes.

ALICE
I see better from here.

(The light flickers)

NURSE
Don't tempt fate.

ALICE
That's exactly what I want to do. Tempt fate. Can you explain to me why fate is so untemptable. Downright obdurate.

NURSE

Perhaps if you put on some powder, a little rouge. You are a woman, you know.

ALICE

Do I look a fright. Tell me.

NURSE

I don't want to be unkind.

ALICE

Tell me.

(The NURSE *fetches the mirror from a drawer—it's a wooden oval on a stick, Italian, ornate, gilt—and puts it in* ALICE*'s hand)*

ALICE

My mirror.

NURSE

Of course you have a mirror.

ALICE

Which, by the way, once belonged to Sarah Bernhardt. Did you know that. Did I ever tell you.

NURSE

I've never been to the theatre.

ALICE

You should. There are inexpensive tickets. Even from the second balcony one can see the whole width of the stage.

NURSE

I never had the time.

ALICE
Did no one ever invite you. Some young man, you should *9*
go with some young man.

NURSE
Someday.

ALICE
Help me.

(The NURSE *rings bell.* M I *and* M II—*they wear white sailor suits—enter and remove the mattresses, stacking them in the rear of the stage)*

NURSE
That's better.

(As mattresses are removed, NURSE *helps* ALICE *to sit up in bed, putting three cusions behind her head.* ALICE *continues to look at herself in the mirror.* M II *exits;* M I *remains near mattresses)*

ALICE
I think I am not dissatisfied with my appearance.

NURSE
Don't be so vain.

*(*NURSE *takes the mirror and looks at herself)*

There is always room for improvement.

ALICE
Of course.

NURSE
A woman can always make herself more attractive.

ALICE

16 I was not thinking of that kind of improvement. *(Begins to turn restlessly in the bed)* Why are you tempting me.

NURSE

I'm helping, you poor motherless girl.

ALICE

Do you know what I once said about Sarah Bernhardt, do you know. *(More and more agitated)* She is a moral abscess, festering with vanity. I did say that.

NURSE

Shall I play some music.

ALICE

Oh, oh.

NURSE

My dear . . .

ALICE

I'm having those thoughts again. *(Thrashing about)* Oh, oh . . .

(NURSE *sits at piano, starts playing passage from Parsifal)*

Maybe I need the matresses again on me. Where. No. I see myself with a knife—no, it's a brick. I see his brains tumbling out of his head. His black Irish brains.

(NURSE *signals* M I, *who takes a syringe from the black bag on a table near the chaise longue and gives* ALICE *an injection)*

Yes, I've done it. I don't care. Let them all hate me. I'm tired of making them sad. Of making them comfortable.

Let them hate me. Oh, the relief. *(She is slowing down)*
Such relief.

11

(NURSE *still playing. Lights dim.* ALICE *sleeps. Black-out. A few moments of music before curtain)*

S C E N E . 3

A younger ALICE *is standing in a shaft of light, center stage, in a long white dress. Light slowly widens, brightens to reveal* FATHER's *study. Books, books.* FATHER *on a ladder*

ALICE
Father.

FATHER
A minute more.

ALICE
Father.

FATHER
Just one.

(He descends the ladder awkwardly, walks stiffly to the desk, sits in his high-backed chair)

ALICE
Father.

FATHER
Yes m'dear.

ALICE
Father.   ß

FATHER
I'm listening Alice. Though I'm busy.

ALICE
Father.

NURSE
My child be reasonable. I'm giving you a portion of my
busy time. As much as you need.

ALICE
Father.

FATHER
I'm listening. I'm patient.

ALICE
Father.

FATHER
I'm sitting down. In the listening position.

ALICE
Father.

FATHER
It's not been hard for you to speak has it. We are a very
eloquent family. I and your four brothers. I was so proud
of you Alice. We, I daresay, are so proud of each other.
Our family.

ALICE
Father.

FATHER

And you the youngest. The baby. Our little girl.

ALICE

Father.

FATHER

My brilliant talkative children. Always chattering, always prattling. Plying your father with questions. Little curious minds. Using big words before you even knew what they meant. Talking, talking.

ALICE

Father.

FATHER

Are you bored m'dear. I have not confined you to women's fiddle-faddle. I gave you the run of the library as I did your brothers.

ALICE

Father.

FATHER

You're merciless m'dear. Do you want to drive me to anger. *(Pause)* You remind me of your mother.

ALICE

Father.

FATHER

(Coldly) She would drive me mad with her silences, too. If you have an accusation to bring against me kindly have the courage to speak out.

(Parsifal *music is heard from off-stage)*

ALICE

I'm very unhappy Mother.

FATHER

Your father m'dear. I'm your father.

ALICE

I'm very unhappy Father.

FATHER

What did you want to ask me.

ALICE

Is it, yes, is it wrong to want to take one's life.

FATHER

Why do you want to grieve those who love you. It's wrong
to cause us so much worry.

ALICE

I've tried Father.

FATHER

If you can try at all then there's no reason ever to stop
trying.

ALICE

Father I've climbed the tree beyond its leaves.

FATHER

In my opinion m'dear you've not even begun to exercise
your considerable talents. This is a more than remarkable
family and you, you know I'm not given to flattery, you
are not the least endowed. Of my five children I would
rate you third in order of genius. Do you hear me. Less
brilliant than two of your brothers, you exceed in brilli-
ance the other two. That middle position would count as
unparalleled genius in almost any other family.

(ALICE has gone to the ladder. She climbs several rungs, scrutinizes books on a high shelf, reaches for one—it is a brick—and slowly dismounts)

You have only to decide to use your abilities, and a vast terrain of fulfillment will open up before you. Even if you are a woman. Yes, I think you are not best suited for family life. You must use that keen mind of yours. Put it to use without fear of intimidating men.

(ALICE stands behind him, holding the brick over his head. FATHER looks around, smiles, holds out his hand. She puts the brick in it)

What a heavy tome. I'd forgot. Volume III. Would you care to borrow it.

(ALICE shakes her head)

It's not without interest. And I know you like to read books that are too difficult for you. Like your brothers you were reading at three.

ALICE
Father what did I tell you.

FATHER
That you're unhappy. Or that you don't want to borrow the book.

ALICE
Listen to me Father. Despair is my normal state.

FATHER
That's what artists say. Maybe you are an artist.

ALICE
An artist is someone who finishes something.

FATHER

My poor child. All that talent. Our talent, the family's
talent. What can I do. You truly want my, my permission. *17*

ALICE

You know what I want.

FATHER

But you're not trying to want something else.

ALICE

Aren't you impressed Father by how unhappy I am.

FATHER

Make an effort. See things differently. With more
distance.

ALICE

Distance.

(ALICE *starts to move to the rear of the stage*)

FATHER

I will tell you a secret daughter.

ALICE

Secret.

FATHER

Nothing that actually occurs is of the slightest
importance.

(ALICE *stops, surprised*)

ALICE

Nothing?

(FATHER *turns his back to audience, unscrews his
right leg, then turns back, brandishing it. Or: he takes*

a hammer and brings it down on his right leg—
thunk—showing it to be wood)

FATHER

You see this wooden contraption that serves me for a leg.
I used to wonder what it would be like to have two real
adult legs. I was a child then, but now I don't. I'm so far
inside the way my life turned out I can't see the edge.

(Lights start to dim. FATHER *hastily reaches in desk*
drawer, takes out miner's lamp, and affixes it to his
forehead. Blackout, except for roving beam of light
from FATHER'S *head)*

Alice?

ALICE

Father.

FATHER

Oh don't. I can't bear it. Where are you. I can't see you.

ALICE

Here Father. You read stories to me. You carried me on
your shoulders.

FATHER

Yes. Have I been a bad father. I told you to think for
yourself. Not a bad father. I didn't tell you to play with
your dolls and leave the books to your brothers. I didn't
put my hand under your dress and ask you not to tell
your mother.

(Beam from lamp finds ALICE *in a swing in rear of*
stage, pushed by M I: M II *standing by. Lights up)*

I asked you questions, showed an interest.

ALICE

Here Father. Waiting for your answer.

FATHER

To what question.

ALICE

May I kill myself Father.

FATHER

Why do you ask me. Could I stop you if you've really set your mind to it. Your willful mind.

(Lights start to dim in front half of stage)

ALICE

Yes. Perhaps. Probably not.

*(Only rear of stage—*ALICE *on the swing—is illuminated)*

FATHER's Voice

I gave you life. I must be for life.

ALICE

My mother gave me life.

FATHER's Voice

Would it help if I were your mother.

(Lights up. FATHER *is now wearing a dress)*

As me again. Ask your mother.

ALICE

Father may I kill myself.

FATHER

Your mother who bore you says no.

ALICE

26 And my father.

FATHER

Your father says you must do what you want.

ALICE

(Dreamily) Want to. Want to . . .

(She is swaying in the swing, not being pushed)

FATHER

I ask only one thing. Do it gently. So as not to distress
those you leave behind . . .

ALICE

Is there a hole I can fall into. Do I have to go to sleep
first.

*(Music up. She flings herself backward, falling into
the arms of* M I *and* M II. *Blackout)*

SCENE 4

ALICE's *bedroom, a different angle (preferably reverse angle) from the set as presented in Scene 2.* ALICE *asleep, under normal amount of bedding.* HARRY *sitting by the bed, holding her hand; he is in his late forties, obese, and wears a caftan.* NURSE *near the door.*

NURSE
She'll wake up soon. She was too excited about your visit.

HARRY
My poor duck.

(ALICE *wakes.* NURSE *tiptoes out*)

ALICE
Oh. How long have you been here. You should have awakened me.

HARRY
I just—

ALICE
Was I sleeping with my mouth open. Did I drool on the pillow.

HARRY

Just arrived only—

ALICE

The pillow is wet. *(Takes his hand, pulling him toward her)* Feel it, feel the pillow. I was drooling, I was disgusting.

(HARRY stands)

HARRY

This is too pitiable. Nurse!

ALICE

No no please Harry, don't, please.

HARRY

You'll stop being hysterical. You'll stop making me feel wretched. *(Sits)* You promise.

ALICE

I promise.

HARRY

You'll be the malicious amusing brilliant little sister that your unworthy brother loves so devotedly.

ALICE

Promise. Look.

(She puts on a red crocheted nightcap. HARRY *laughs)*

HARRY

And what has my dear rabbit been thinking, safe and protected in her lair, while her owl was out in the world suffering the slings arrows et cetera.

ALICE

Harry what's your idea finally why I am like this. And don't tell me because I'm so sensitive.

HARRY

But I'm not. *(Warmly)* I think it's because you're so 23
intelligent.

ALICE

I don't think I'm intelligent at all, that's the truth. If you
want the truth.

HARRY

Ah mouse. You wrong yourself. Perhaps you're the most
intelligent of us all.

ALICE

Don't mock me. Don't mouse me.

HARRY

I'm not.

ALICE

Don't patronize me.

HARRY

I'm not, dear heart.

ALICE

You know you don't think I'm more intelligent than you
are Harry.

HARRY

What is intelligence but a form, the form, of intensity?
And, yes dear heart, I'm not your match in the extraor-
dinary intensity of your will and your personality. That
would create enormous practical problems of life, if you
chose to live in what is called, in a permanent fit of
overvaluation, the real world. Your disastrous, your
tragic—

ALICE

Tragic.

HARRY

"Her tragic health was in a manner the only solution for her of the problem of life—as it suppressed the lament of equality, reciprocity, etc."

ALICE

What a terrible thing to say. Why should equality, reciprocity be more of a problem for me than for you. Tell me. Are you saying this of me.

HARRY

Not yet. It's what I will say of you two years after you have died, at the age of forty-four—

ALICE

Don't tell me.

HARRY

Of course not.

(He leans forward to caress her cheek)

ALICE

No no I don't mind. I find I am more curious than I thought. Well let's have it all. Do I, I mean will I, tenses are strangely potent aren't they, commit suicide.

HARRY

You don't take your life.

ALICE

After all that talk. I should be ashamed of myself.

HARRY

(Smiling tenderly) Yes.

ALICE

So I didn't commit suicide. And I'll have, I gather from
your discreet silence, a real illness. Much preferable to
this tiresome neurasthenia. I never quite saw myself as
Elizabeth Barrett being unable to envisage for myself
either the literary gift or the ardent rescuer. *(Pauses)*
Cancer.

HARRY

Alas.

ALICE

There is agony I've been told.

HARRY

Don't brood my dear. It is not possible that your admi-
rable spirit, your heroism, will fail you.

ALICE

Did Father also think my tragic health, as you call it, a
good solution.

HARRY

Will call it.

ALICE

Did he. A good solution. Did he.

(She knoicks over the lamp on her night table)

HARRY

How can I know, my dear. Father is dead. I never detected
in him our bleakness of vision.

(He rings bell)

You know what a congenital optimist Father was. It is
we who see things with such shadows.

(M I and M II enter. Sweep up lamp. Put one mattress on ALICE. *Exit)*

ALICE
I'm not really tired.

HARRY
Shall I call your sainted nurse.

ALICE
No, no, don't begin to go. You promised me. Have you brought some chapters of the new book. Will you tell me some gossip. Will you—

(He reaches out to stroke her forehead)

HARRY
But take your laudanum.

ALICE
Yes. It makes me dream.

(He offers her the bottle and a spoon. She takes the medicine)

Harry answer me this truthfully.

HARRY
Of course dear heart, aren't you my precious turtle.

ALICE
Harry did you ever use, I think they say eat, but isn't it smoke, opium. Now don't lie. Tell me.

HARRY
Of course not.

ALICE

Never. Not even wanted to. Harry! Harry. Look at me. Look at your Alice.

HARRY

(Laughs) Well I did envisage it. But no. Never. I'm not, like our Wim, one for experimenting with the mind.

ALICE

I would, if I could.

HARRY

Why.

ALICE

Dead fish have to swim.

HARRY

I see no dead fish, I see a limpid stream, a spontaneous irrigator of which the snags of doubt have never interrupted nor made turbid the easily flowing current.

ALICE

You quote me. Yes dear brother you quote me. I don't know whether to be embarrassed or flattered.

HARRY

Have I ever ceased to tell you how much I admire your eloquence.

ALICE

My resignation.

HARRY

But how you have struggled dear heart. What you call resignation I call a newfound victory: that you, even you, can allow that agitated spirit some rest.

ALICE

28 Resignation. Defeat.

HARRY

No.

ALICE

Exhaustion. "Long ceaseless strain and tension have worn out all aspiration save the one for Rest! The shaping period is past and one is fitted to every limitation through the long custom of surrender."

HARRY

Dear heart!

ALICE

I can't help it. Now I'm quoting myself. Oh.

(HARRY *looks about anxiously*)

Oh. Oh.

(M I *and* M II *enter swiftly. Another mattress*)

HARRY

Be calm dear heart.

ALICE

How sick one gets of being good and how much, oh, I would respect myself if I could burst out and make everyone wretched for twenty-four hours.

HARRY

Only twenty-four hours.

ALICE

Ah you are a man, while my thoughts women's thoughts

are diminutive. You're right. Twenty-four years. *(Laughs)* Twenty-four lifetimes.

HARRY

Try it. Maybe you're not as good as you think. Maybe you make us wretched quite regularly.

ALICE

Yes, perhaps I'm not good. Just stupid. Now Father is gone and we live here rather than there though I live in a room and I see you when you're so kind as to visit me and I'm dependent for mental stimulation on Nurse, well, is it any wonder if I'm getting stupid. I have these grand thoughts, moments when my mind is flooded by a luminous wave that fills me with the sense of potency of vitality of understanding, and I feel I've pierced the mystery of the universe, and then it's time for an emetic or to have my hair brushed or a sheet changed. Or these mattresses . . . I think I've reached some singular peak from which all is clear and it turns out to be just one of the countless ways in which I "go off" as Father always called it . . .

HARRY

Let me remove one of the mattresses. I can do it myself.

ALICE

Don't breathe so hard, you need more exercise. Listen I've botched it. Now the question is how to end.

HARRY

I told you what the end was. We're not going to talk about it anymore.

ALICE

I can talk about what I like. It can have a different ending. Perhaps I shall have a narrow escape. Perhaps everything will change at the last minute.

HARRY

30 You're insisting.

(Gets up)

Don't.

ALICE

I told you about the conversation with Father. I was twenty.

HARRY

Many times.

ALICE

I'm not asking you for permission Harry. You've given me so much.

HARRY

I would never have answered as he did.

(Sits)

You're not required to spare us distress. *(He is fighting back tears)* Don't spare us distress. I think you deserve to outlive us all. You only have to want to.

ALICE

Ah. Wanting. I've been told that before.

HARRY

A matter of self-respect.

ALICE

Which is wanting.

HARRY

You play with words dear heart.

ALICE

It is an answer. I didn't mean anything so hand-wringing.

HARRY

Were you ever happy as a child. I mean up to when. You must have been. Nobody starts out in despair from the very beginning. You must have been. Why don't I remember. *(Tearful)* I've known you all my life.

ALICE

No. I've known you all my life. You're older. Harry please don't weep.

HARRY

(Dries eyes) I know I cannot make you like to live, or regard death with less indiscreet familiarity.

ALICE

Stop. Tell me about yourself.

HARRY

Now who is comforting whom.

ALICE

Well I am a woman and that is a woman's job, to comfort and reassure men, even from the bed, sickbed deathbed birthbed, to which the man has come, on tiptoe, to visit and comfort, is it not.

HARRY

How bitter you are my sister. Father always said you were bitter.

ALICE

Not so bitter as not to be able to laugh at myself. At you. Even at Father . . .

(HARRY signals for another mattress)

Yes I was cold.

HARRY

You look more comfortable now. You can't go off.

ALICE

Why are you so fat Harry. Oh. Who said that.

HARRY

Sleep, sleep dear heart.

ALICE

Not yet. Lean closer Harry. Tell me a story. Bring me the world. I want to laugh with you, covet with you, be cast down with you, feel superior with you. My swan.

HARRY

My own darling girl.

(He leans forward. Music up. Lights dim very slowly)

SCENE 5

Veranda or sun room. Large tree-like plant. Long table with full white tablecloth, teapot, tray, cups, and saucers. White-painted wicker chairs grouped at one end of the table. MARGARET *in one of the chairs, holding a cup and saucer, reading. She has on a hat and is robust, homely, appealing. In another chair* KUNDRY, *head down, asleep.* EMILY—*frail, in a shift—enters.*

EMILY
Margaret. Don't get up.

MARGARET
Are we early.

EMILY
Tenderness is always timely.

MARGARET
I think I'm early. Perhaps you are punctual.

EMILY
Waiting is a long hello.

MARGARET

34 She should drink lemon tea. Mine is with milk. Am I
supposed to offer you something. But I do not consider
myself the hostess.

EMILY

(Looking at KUNDRY*)* Will she wake up.

MARGARET

It depends o nus. On the need.

EMILY

I'd like there to be others.

MARGARET

I mean to be of help. I think I *can* be helpful.

EMILY

The need is like a flower, and I have prepared my flower
smile.

(MARGARET, *sipping her tea, has put the book on her
knee. It falls to the floor;* EMILY *leans over and returns
it to her)*

MARGARET

Grazie.

EMILY

Who else then.

MARGARET

Why do you want there to be others. I should think we're
more than enough.

EMILY

I shall always defer to you.

MARGARET
Oh please. Don't tell me that you find me intimidating. ✄

EMILY
Yes. But what pleasure I get from defying my fears!

MARGARET
Our fears our griefs are not the point here as far as I understand.

(ALICE *is carried in by* M I *and* M II)

Ah. Here's our girl.

(ALICE *is set down in the chair at the end of the table; her legs are covered with a paisley shawl.* MARGARET *draws her chair closer*)

Alice, Emily was saying she found it intimidating to be alone with me. Don't you hate it when someone says that to you.

ALICE
I'm sure Emily meant it as a compliment.

EMILY
I didn't say it. I admitted it. Which is another season.

MARGARET
(To ALICE*)* Don't you cringe when someone says that to you.

ALICE
What a beautiful day. It would be preposterous for anyone to say such a thing to me.

MARGARET
Nonsense. Of course it has been said to and of you. You're ambushed. Either you take it as a compliment, and then

you're straddling your flatterer whether you want to or
not. Or you start reassuring, groveling really, to put the
other at ease.

36

(EMILY *moves toward the door*)

Emily where are you going.

ALICE
Emily.

EMILY
I brought flowers. I did bring them. Wait.

(She exits)

MARGARET
Do you think I offended her. I'm truly sorry. Sometimes
I have acted on a strong impulse and could not analyze
what passed in my mind. I acted what was in my character. It is a terrible world. It was hard to be a woman
known, among other attributes, for her homeliness.

ALICE
You may complain to me. Do.

MARGARET
I'm sorry if I offended her.

ALICE
She'll return, she promised. Let's take this moment
alone. I do admire that you had the courage to live to
write to be enthusiastic, to walk about the world. I do
admire you.

MARGARET
I was an embarrassment to others. And then to the relief
of many I died.

ALICE
I'm an embarrassment to myself. *(Laughs)* And you
wanted to live. Look what it took to subdue you. Those *37*
were mighty waters.

(MARGARET *sighs*)

I'm sorry. I don't mean to remind you so lightheartedly.
I think about death so much, death is such a familiar,
consoling thought, I forget how weighty it is when you're
out in the world. *(Pause)* I live so lightly I need to be held
down.

MARGARET
It was a terrible ending. I tried to save my baby. We
drowned within a hundred yards of the land.

ALICE
Forgive me. I shouldn't make personal remarks.

MARGARET
I do, whenever I can.

(*Looking at* KUNDRY)

I do think it's rude of her to go on sleeping. But I'm trying
to sympathize.

ALICE
Let's not wake her. Two is my favorite size for a party.
And let's not be sad. I want to arrive at a more buoyant
conclusion.

MARGARET
Would you like some tea. I think I am the only one here
with any manners.

ALICE

38 Lemon tea.

MARGARET

I knew that's what you would ask for. I said to Emily that while I prefer tea with milk, you would—

(Looks in teapot)

But there isn't any and I shouldn't have offered because I am not and do not want to be the hostess.

(KUNDRY raises her head—she is disheveled, has wild hair, etc.—and speaks as if still sleeping)

KUNDRY

You might as well say I sleep because I am suffering as that I am suffering because I am asleep.

ALICE

Kundry.

KUNDRY

Who has called.

ALICE

No one who means you harm.

KUNDRY

Why have I been awakened. I want to sleep.

(She lays her head down again on the table; sleeps)

MARGARET

I don't mean to frustrate you.

ALICE
What.

MARGARET
The tea. I wish there were tea. But I think it is not for
me to regret or to provide. Then shall we have a pipe.

ALICE
Yes. Yes. Exactly what I was thinking.

(Rings bell. M I *and* M II *wheel in a dozen or so
mattresses and a tray-table with paraphernalia for
smoking opium: two large hookahs, etc. Faint Parsifal music from off-stage)*

Let's not wait for Emily. Are we being naughty. I don't
think this particular pleasure would be good for Emily.

(They laugh)

Most imprudent.

(ALICE *leans toward* MARGARET, *then pulls away
abruptly)*

Oh I think I am siding with mediocrity. I am betraying
her or myself or someone. Oh. Is this who I want to talk
to.

MARGARET
Yes.

*(*M I *and* M II *have set two stacks of three mattresses
on the floor, keeping the rest to the side)*

It does not I think require genius to live.

ALICE

40 *(Still agitated)* I am betraying myself.

MARGARET

(Dryly) How inconvenient to be two people. The possibility of betrayal does in that case I fear suggest itself.

(She pauses, looks at ALICE expectantly)

ALICE

(Suddenly relaxing) You are right of course. I am taking myself much too seriously. Oh. *(Laughs)* I'm still two am I not. I'm afraid I have never been gifted for having or even attending a party.

(M II drops something, making a loud noise)

KUNDRY

(Raising her head, eyes closed) Why have I been awakened.

(MARGARET taps KUNDRY on the shoulder, looks at ALICE, shakes her head)

MARGARET

Oh *this* lost soul.

ALICE

From my limited experience of parties—

MARGARET

Don't denigrate yourself. The first rule.

ALICE

I was going to say that I'm not prepared to say she's being rude. I'm so sorry for her.

MARGARET

She will eventually find us interesting I wager.

(M I *and* M II *install* MARGARET *and* ALICE *on the mattresses with their hookahs. Music up. Lights lower)*

ALICE
I do love lying down don't you.

MARGARET
(Languid voice) I was very active. *(Inhales)* But now I'm not myself.

ALICE
(Laughs) You see. You too. Two of you. It's always like that when you think.

MARGARET
(Dreamily) Not myself. I'm adapting to my environment.

ALICE
(Sighing) I've never seen Rome. And now I never shall.

MARGARET
It's just as you imagine. That beautiful. Are you imaginging it.

ALICE
I suppose you are against suicide.

MARGARET
Never seen the point. We dic too soon anyway.

ALICE
(Sitting up) We've abandoned Kundry too. Who I'm sure would be more comfortable lying down with us.

MARGARET
Even Kundry, you will note, does not kill herself.

(ALICE *settles back on the mattress; inhales smoke)*

ALICE

42 I wanted advice. From a woman I could respect. I've always sought advice from men.

MARGARET

People were always giving me advice, for my own good. Truth was, they did not want me to embarrass them.

ALICE

Exactly.

(They laugh)

I don't have a sister.

MARGARET

Women despair differently. I've observed that. We can be very stoical.

ALICE

I don't know whether to feel more or less.

(She sits, refills hookah)

I'm at a turning. *(Inhales)* Do you think Emily will return. Do you think Kundry will wake up. I realize I rather liked the idea of a party. Feeling less perhaps.

MARGARET

Thinking doesn't help? I always found it helped.

ALICE

Thinking.

MARGARET

Unhappiness may be only a mistake. A mental mistake, that you could still undo.

ALICE
Retrace my steps. Oh. But I can't walk. *(Becoming agi-* 43
tated) You see I can't walk.

(Knocks over her hookah)

I'm feeling very strange. Is it this? Don't you feel strange.

(Sound of waves)

MARGARET
I'm not susceptible. Wish I were *(Sighs)* but I'm too
practical.

(Stands)

Always have my feet on the ground. *(Laughs)* When
they're not in the water.

ALICE
I have to be calm. Help me.

MARGARET
Good. You're becoming excited.

ALICE
I must be calm. When I crossed the Atlantic it was No-
vember. The sea was calm. But I never left my cabin.
Shortly after the ship sailed I had what Father called one
of my nervous attacks. I never left my cabin. Miss Loring
was with me. Harry met the boat at Liverpool. Two stout
sailors carried me ashore and I spent a week recuperating
in a Liverpool hotel, attended by a maid Harry had
brought, and a nurse, and Miss Loring. Then Harry took
me to London and installed me in lodgings near Picca-
dilly near his own rooms.

MARGARET
You crossed the Atlantic and never left your cabin?

ALICE
50 Recumbent.

MARGARET
The sea was, there was no, the sea—

ALICE
Calm.

MARGARET
You didn't want to see anything.

ALICE
Don't reproach me.

(Light change. EMILY *enters with flowers. She distributes them)*

You left us Emily. We waited for you. That doesn't seem fair.

EMILY
The pain deserved a blank.

ALICE*I did think this was a party you were giving for me. And so I thought no doubt mistakenly that I could count on a minimum of—*

(She sees EMILY *at the table reaching for the teapot)*

You know there isn't any tea.

*(*ALICE *pours herself tea, stands sipping it)*

MARGARET
(To ALICE*)* I'm beginning to worry about you. Truly worry.

ALICE
What do you mean.

(EMILY *sits demurely on a mattress*)

MARGARET
I do question the need, I suppose I mean the wisdom, but
of course it's in the end a matter of common sense, when,
by asking Emily as well, you—

ALICE
What have you got against Emily, Margaret. *(To* EMILY*)*
You don't mind if I ask Margaret to say what she means.

EMILY
No.

ALICE
Be blunt.

MARGARET
I always am. But now I wonder—

ALICE
No please.

EMILY
Yes.

MARGARET
(After a pause) You're not I think giving life a chance.

ALICE
Because I invited Emily.

EMILY
One can't think about death steadily any more than one
can stare at the sun. I think about it slant.

MARGARET
46 You like that tone don't you.

ALICE
(To margaret) I suppose I do. *(To* EMILY*)* I think your interest in death is more interesting than mine.

MARGARET
I thought we were here to talk about life.

EMILY
Death is the lining. The lines.

ALICE
I remember when my mother died—

> (MOTHER *enters; all in white. White full coat, carries white umbrella, wears white gloves)*

Oh my god. I didn't invite her. I never invited her.

> (MOTHER *moves toward table)*

MARGARET
Alice.

EMILY
Alice.

KUNDRY
(Lifts head, eyes closed) Who called.

ALICE
(Air of terror) She'll stay and then we can't talk.

MARGARET
You can talk.

(Moves to stand protectively near ALICE*)*

EMILY
You are talking.

ALICE
I'm going to pretend that I don't mind. Then perhaps she'll go away.

MOTHER
Oh your poor mother.

(Stands behind chair next to KUNDRY, *who has her head on the table)*

ALICE
(Whispering) It's my mother. She's dead too.

MARGARET
You didn't invite her.

ALICE
(Whispering) Certainly not. *(Pause)* Mother.

MOTHER
Oh your poor mother.

ALICE
Sit down Mother. *(Whispering, to* MARGARET *and* EMILY*)* I have to invite her now. It would be rude not to.

MOTHER
I can't say I'm observing it but I'm not ignoring it either.

MARGARET
(Loud whisper) What's she talking about.

ALICE

48 Me. I suppose. *(To* MOTHER*)* Sit down please. *(To* MAR-
GARET *and* EMILY*)* You see. I don't mean anything I say.
(Pause) She was always out of range.

(MOTHER *attempts to sit. Crowds* KUNDRY, *who
whimpers, flails about; won't let her sit)*

KUNDRY

What day is it. What year is it. How dare she.

MARGARET

Couldn't you just turn it upside down. Throw it down a
hole. Tip it sideways. And let all those hard griefs slither
away like curds turned out of their dish.

MOTHER

I can't say I'm walking but I'm not limping either.

(She has stopped trying to wrest a chair from KUNDRY.
Opens umbrella. Looks up)

KUNDRY

At this table there's no room.

MOTHER

I never insisted.

(MOTHER *exits)*

KUNDRY

(Eyes still shut) I think Kundry has saved you.

(Rocks back and forth)

MARGARET

A chastening apparition.

ALICE

I remember when my mother died my youngest brother
said that we have all been educated by Father to feel that
death was the only reality and that life was simply an
experimental thing.

MARGARET

An experiment. An experiment. An experiment.

ALICE

Are you making fun of me.

(MARGARET *sighs, shakes her head*)

KUNDRY

(Still rocking) It is hard to save anyone. But that is all we
desire.

ALICE

He said, my brother said, that we feel that we are more
near to her now than ever before, simply because she is
already at the goal to which we all cheerfully bend our
steps.

EMILY

Cheerfully is a lovely, lethal word.

ALICE

He said, my youngest brother said, after our mother died:
"The last two weeks have been the happiest I have
known."

(*Looks at* MARGARET *and* EMILY, *then starts to
laugh*)

Yes it is mad isn't it. But you see how difficult it was for
us. Father had high standards. We were not supposed to
be, well, like the others.

MARGARET

Lived. Lived. Lived. Yes I lived, and yes I did not find it
so difficult. I went out on the deck. Nothing could have
made me renounce standing on the deck, feeling the wind
on my face, pushing through my clothes.

EMILY

I've never been on a boat.

KUNDRY

(Still rocking) My horse. My legs.

MARGARET

(To EMILY, *in a kindly tone)* I know this can't mean much
to *you*. But I think—at least I said, I did say: Those have
not lived who have not seen Rome.

ALICE

Ah travel.

KUNDRY

(Rocking) The Pope. He can bless, but can he save, but
can he damn. No.

EMILY

It's a question of scale. To me it was an adventure to cross
the village lane.

(MYRTHA *enters. Long white dress, chiffon veil, baby
wings, headband with flowers, etc. A kind of Dervish
twirling step. Music from Giselle)*

ALICE

Did I invite her. Who is it. It's not— Ah Myrtha. Come
and join us.

(MYRTHA *stops)*

What's wrong.

MYRTHA
I'd rather not lie down.

MARGARET
No one will force you.

ALICE
Do you want to stand.

MYRTHA
Actually I'm not supposed to lie down.

(Resumes twirling)

In the forest. In the glade. I live in the forest. That's where
the graves are. He brings flowers.

(Stops again)

What beautiful flowers.

MARGARET
We were talking about unhappiness.

(Sits at the table, opposite KUNDRY*)*

MYRTHA
(To ALICE*)* I think there is a man who has broken your
heart.

ALICE
My father perhaps.

MYRTHA
We could kill him. Then you would have to kill yourself.
Beautiful flowers.

(Resumes twirling)

ALICE

I always thought a man would crush me. He would put a pillow over my face. I wanted a man's weight on my body. But then I couldn't move.

(EMILY stands, helps ALICE to stand; MARGARET leaves table to help. Together they bring ALICE to her seat at the table)

MARGARET

I can understand your not wanting it. Of course you feel pinned down. It's good. And then you get up afterward.

(M I and M II have entered. M I sets a pot of tea on the table)

MYRTHA

He can't atone. You shouldn't forgive him.

(M I and M II gather up and remove most of the mattresses and the hookahs)

ALICE

I remember a young man, Julian, he was a music student, a friend of my brother, of Harry I mean. He and Harry were always together. But he liked me. I used to imagine that we could go swimming together. I used to imagine his body.

MYRTHA

Flowers. Revenge.

EMILY

It's a winsome longing.

MARGARET
My idea is this. Want what you are capable of, and what
you are capable of wanting, and be *completely* clear on *53*
the matter and: live according to it.

ALICE
Life is not just a question of courage.

MARGARET
But it is.

EMILY
(To ALICE*)* I think you are quite brave.

MYRTHA
How can you stand to be inside. In a room.

ALICE
You don't know the fearful things I see when I close my
eyes. I have to die so I don't see the monstrous things.

MARGARET
I see terrible things when I open my eyes.

MYRTHA
In a room. In a tomb.

KUNDRY
(Reaches across table convulsively; looks into ALICE*'s eyes)*
Give me your hand.

ALICE
What do you see?

  (Extends her hand. KUNDRY *takes it, brings it to her
  forehead, kisses it, then flings it back)*

KUNDRY

Kindry's visions are the most terrible. Most terrible. I must be punished. My body wants—but I don't. It wants, it's so big, I can't I don't want, he wants, he makes me, but I want to, I want to first . . .

(Starting to fall asleep)

First I'll want, if they let me, when I don't feel . . .

ALICE

Poor soul.

KUNDRY

(Waking again) Why have I been awakened. I want to sleep.

ALICE

Please don't become, well . . . crazed. We mean you no harm. We have the most sisterly respect for your suffering.

MARGARET

However retrograde.

EMILY

I trust that my flowers have the good grace to be seared by our shouts.

KUNDRY

Why did you wake me.

ALICE

I told you.

*(*KUNDRY *stares uncomprehendingly)*

MARGARET

She told you. But there may have been a mistake.

ALICE

Please don't be angry. You needn't have come if you
really didn't want to.

EMILY

It wasn't an order, that's what she's saying. But it was a
wind.

KUNDRY

Oh, oh.

MARGARET

There's a mattress. Lie down.

ALICE

Do you want anything to drink or eat. We did not offer
before because we thought you preferred—

(KUNDRY *is very agitated.* MARGARET *and* EMILY
help her lie down on a mattress)

EMILY

Let her sleep.

MARGARET

Here. Some tea.

(KUNDRY *groans, refuses the tea)*

ALICE

I was, we are, wrong to have disturbed her.

KUNDRY

Sleep, sleep . . .

(She sleeps, or seems to)

MARGARET
She'll be of no more use now.

EMILY
Shhhh . . .

MARGARET
Is this sleep different from when she was at the table. I don't see why we have to whisper. It's not I think that she sleeps so soundly.

ALICE
Yes she wakes when she wants to.

MYRTHA
I like being aware.

(Picks up sheaf of flowers and dances with them)

KUNDRY
(Opening her eyes) There's an answer. Which is . . .

(Her eyes start to close; she makes an effort)

There's a question.

ALICE
We've decided to ask you straight out why you sleep.

KUNDRY
Because my body is heavy. The innocent boy came and I tried to corrupt him. To make him desire me. He did desire me, but more as a mother than as a lover. And, still, he resisted me. So I felt ashamed. I fell down a bottomless well of shame. I'm still falling. How tiring. Oblivion.

MYRTHA

Exact your revenge. Men making women into whores
and angels, how can you believe that. Have you no self-
respect.

MARGARET

My husband was a boy and, unlike me, an exceedingly
delicate person. I felt safe with him. And we had a child.
I think he would have proved an excellent father, though
he could not speculate about it, or indeed about anything.

EMILY

I stayed home and wrote. My brother fornicated. I was
in a room with blue trim. I could see an orchard from
my window. He came in, he had a goatee. Death. The
frogs were singing. They have such pretty lazy times. How
nice to be a frog! When the best is gone I know that other
things are not of consequence. The heart wants what it
wants or else it does not care.

KUNDRY

I'm still falling. And I am not allowed to the end.

EMILY

One would prefer to look behind at a pain than to see it
coming.

KUNDRY

Sleep . . .

ALICE

Is she sleeping.

EMILY

The day begins whenever it can.

MYRTHA

It's as if she were drugged. We could make her stand.

(Lifts teapot, as if to pour it on KUNDRY)

ALICE

Oh be careful.

EMILY

We could comb out the knots in her hair.

MARGARET

She isn't sleeping, she's hiding.

(MARGARET *and* EMILY, *after pulling the reluctant*
MYRTHA *down with them, to help, kneel around*
KUNDRY, *arranging her arms, straightening her legs)*

MYRTHA

(To ALICE) Doesn't she make you want to race about.
Not even a little bit.

*(Stands. Begins doing warm-up exercises, using the
table edge as a barre)*

MARGARET

Yes!

MYRTHA

You see, Alice, Margaret and I agree. *(Pause)* Come.

(Holds out her hand to ALICE)

ALICE

(Irritably) I fail to see what Kundry's preference for the
lying position has to do with my own.

MYRTHA
We're talking about helplessness. We're invoking revolt.

EMILY
An ill heart, like a body, has its more comfortable days
as well as its days of pain.

ALICE
Is this your advice. But that's what everyone says. They
tell me to get up. Get up they say *(Pause)* Or they've
stopped telling me to get up because they still want me
to, but they've given up thinking I ever will.

MYRTHA
When we say it it's different.

ALICE
It's still the same answer. I'm disappointed.

EMILY
Orders fall, questions rise.

MARGARET
Shall we take a vote.

ALICE
You do make me laugh all of you. I know someone is
trying to be logical.

MYRTHA
Just move, you'll discover. The strength you don't know.

(MYRTHA
resumes twirling very slowly. EMILY *still sits beside* KUN-
DRY, *stroking her hair.* MARGARET *retrieves her book)*

ALICE
You're asking me to dance.

EMILY

You are moving. But the velocity of the ill is that of the snail.

(KUNDRY *opens her eyes, partly sits up*)

KUNDRY

It's a cycle. Dejection Revolt Sleep Reconciliation.

MYRTHA

A circle. Just move.

MARGARET

It's a council. We're here to advise you.

ALICE

Advice. It's enough if you console me. If you kindle my imagination. Draw close.

(Sees them hesitating)

But don't think I'm jealous of your attentions to Kundry. Closer. Whisper to me. Tell me what you know. I feel so small.

EMILY

What I know is so small . . .

MYRTHA

I wish I could stay . . .

MARGARET

You already know what you want to know . . .

KUNDRY

Sleep . . .

(MYRTHA *leaves*)

ALICE
Oh stay.

(Turns to the others)

I disappointed her.

(M I and M II come in with stretcher and take KUNDRY *away on it)*

MARGARET
I'm going to see Emily part of the way back. Opposites attract.

ALICE
And who am I the opposite of. Don't be disappointed with me.

MARGARET
We'll come again.

EMILY
We'll write to each other.

ALICE
I'll be here. In my place. *(Laughs)* You know where to find me. Oh Margaret when I think of all the places you've been. And I stay in my lair. I'd wanted to ask you about Rome. About the layers. And the shock. Just a few more minutes. Emily won't be bored.

(Lights are dimming)

Emily. Margaret.

(Blackout)

SCENE 6

ALICE, *in portion of bedroom magnified so she seems very small. Sitting on a child's chair, stage front. Only half the giant bed, with a gigantic red pillow, is visible behind her.*

ALICE

My mind. I can travel with my mind. With my mind I'm in Rome, where Margaret lived. Where Harry descended. I've put aside their books. My turn now. I walk on the streets. That's the power of a mind. I see the washer-women. The palaces. I smell the garlic. Orange peels in the gutter. I hear the bells of the nearby convent. People are bawling and gesturing, trying to sell you things. Children beg, mothers with children beg. They're professionals, I suppose. Carriages go smashing past me. Not smashing, I meant to say rumbling. I'd watch the excavations. There's still so much more to dig up. Ruins are beautiful I think. They're so—speaking. Don't you think. And the marvelous sunsets, burnishing the ocher walls. I'd see that too, I do see it. Monuments. In my mind. It's supposed to be the most beautiful city in the world, although other people say Paris. And some say Venice, but Venice has too many odors, and Venice makes everyone think of death. But Rome makes you think of survival, and that thought would be in my mind when I'm in Rome. In my mind, in that beauty. If I would see all that beauty

I know it would make me very happy. It would fill me. I would write about it in my diary, I would sketch it—yes, one more tourist recording her impressions. I would be very humble. Who am I, compared with Rome. I come to see Rome, it doesn't come to see me. It can't move. *(Pause)* In my mind—here: in Rome—I know I would like Rome. I do like it, I'm thrilled by it, exalted when I travel there, in my mind. It's everything I imagine. But then I am only imagining, that's right. But that's a mind. The power of a mind. With my mind I can see, I can hold all that in my mind. Everyone says it's so beautiful. I've looked at the pictures, the engravings. Yes, Piranesi. I receive letters from people in Rome who tell me how happy they are. You know what I mean by people: foreigners. If I would see all that beauty I know it would make me very happy, but I don't know how I would separate from it. When would I have had enough. I would become so attached to Rome I would want to stay there forever. I would never have enough. I would walk on the streets and cross the squares and there would always be another street, another view. Perspectives, colonnades. The obelisks. And the cats, homeless, impudent. Shadows at night and the hot breeze. Harry told me about a girl who went to the Coliseum at night and caught pneumonia and died. It's dangerous to be alone—she wasn't, she went there with a man—but I like to think of being alone, in my mind I'm alone in Rome, even though it's a city where women are harassed when walking about alone, I can be alone there, quite invulnerable, altogether safe— in my mind, in Rome. Alone I loiter in the churches, crossing myself furtively. I want to cross myself, it feels right, but I don't want anyone to see me. How shocked Father would be. Wim not. *(Pause)* You see I am not Catholic of course—and my mind is, I dare flatter myself, relatively free of superstitions, including Popish ones. *(A dry laugh)* Of course, I flatter myself. My mind must be chock full of superstitions. Ones I don't even know about. The superstitions of this new time. With my mind I am

hinged to the time I live in whether I like it or not. *(Pause)*
It's the power of a mind to know that, too. It takes me
quite past myself. I can be very big and see myself quite
small, and it's still me; in my mind. In this new ugly time.
Is it ugly. Yes. I can't help feeling that, in my mind. Am
I a snob in my mind, in Rome, like all those visiting
Americans abasing themselves before Italians with titles.
Am I nostalgic for another Rome, the one before this one,
which is the only one I can know, if I were to go there,
though I haven't. Do I, even when I come to Rome, a
novice in these sympathies, ally myself with the past. Like
Margaret and Harry, with their idyllic memories of a
separate, papal Rome. Irrevocably past. Perhaps. We are
always looking for the past, especially when we travel.
And I am in my mind, traveling, and the mind is the past,
and the mind is Rome. And this time is in the mind, too.
I will not fall into the gulf of history. I will cling to the
side. Because I'm in my mind *(She starts to rock)*, which
is like a boat or a chair or a bed or a tree. Or a rope
bridge. And in my mind I can be high up, too. There are
vantage points in the mind, in the world. A panorama of
roofs and domes, clear-cut against the Roman sky. I see
that, from a hill, from my mind, though Rome is not a
city one wants to see from afar, except in one's mind, like
Aeneas. No, not like Aeneas, he didn't really see anything, he just plunged. Whereas I can have an overview,
in my mind. Held in the beak of a bird, I'm flying over
Rome, it rushes past me, the S of the Tiber, the hills, the
fountains, and tiny carriages, drawn by brightly capari-
soned toy horses, prancing over warm stones. In Rome,
in my mind, there is a whole world underneath, subter-
rean chambers, lost foundations, dead rooms with floor-
wide mosaics whose tiny cubes of color hiss in the dark-
ness, cloaca maxima. In the mind. One can't see everything. But on the surface there's so much. In Rome
wherever you turn there's another view, another stained
wall, all that you don't see, the walls hung with silk, piano
nobile, the hidden gardens, monsters of stone. So much
stone; this stony lump in my breast. Broken stones, which

means broken writing. The letters are all capitals. Their authors thought themselves very important, which is what makes you important: work of the mind. Who built, who made, who gave, who honored, who lies—almost always I can make out what it says. There is Latin in my mind, too, which Father put there, as he had put it in the minds of my brothers. He could not, he said, do less for me; for my mind. They made, they claimed, they died, they are still remembered. But remembered wrong, which is what remembering is. The views push on, one view translates into another, there are walls, doors, arches, terraces, another view, another change, but it's still the same place: Rome—in my mind. I can go as far as I want, I can do what I can't do, what I shouldn't do, in my mind. Something troubles me, I ache, an urchin is trailing me, curly hair, rags, sores on his arms, yellow mucus on his upper lip, he tugs at my skirt, he holds out his hand, if you give to one you should give to all is what the visitor is told, sagely. The child, there is something wrong with his thumb, he still holds out his hand, the child is in my mind too, the life I do not lead, the suffering I do not know, how can I dare I suffer not suffer for that. I pull away from the child or I give him everything I have or I give him one round warm coin, everything I do, in my mind, is wrong. And he vanishes, because I don't know what to do with him, for him, in my mind. Leaving an ache. And his twisted blackened little thumb, he's left his thumb in my mind. I keep moving, it is such a pleasure to move; in my mind. And when the church bells ring, it will be time, time for some people, better than consulting watches. But I don't go indoors, though all manner of invitations have been extended to me, perhaps only out of politeness, I stay outdoors, in my mind, in the sun, and I walk freely, my legs like stout stilts, I cross bridges, the river is shallow, I watch the low-flying black birds boiling above the bridges at sunset, the angel watches from the top of the angel's castle. I walk vigorously, dressed properly for whatever the weather is, it is not often a trial, not feeling in any way diminished by the grandeur of the spectacle, for the mind has its own swellings and diminishings, and who is to say what is the right size. Or the right age. How old am I. I won't say how old anything is. Rome is famous for being very old. I won't say how big or how small anything is. My mind doesn't have a size. One size fits all.

(Slow fade)

SCENE 7

ALICE's bedroom, another angle. Night light. ALICE asleep.

ALICE, snoring, turns in the bed, then is quiet again. Sound of the lock on the doors to the balcony being forced open; or perhaps a pane of glass being cut out with an awl, after which a hand reaches in to unlock the doors from the inside.

A YOUNG MAN, around eighteen, shabbily dressed, pushes open the doors. He has a coil of rope and a canvas sack on his shoulder, and carries a lantern, a small bag of tools, and a small carpetbag. Stares for a long moment at ALICE in bed, sleeping; hesitates, listens to her breathing. Then he enters, puts down the lantern, removes his shoes. On tiptoe he goes to take small ornate Empire clock, puts it in the sack. Rifles desk drawer, puts something in the carpetbag; from top drawer of the chest he pulls out what could be a brooch and a necklace and puts them in the bag. His back is to ALICE.

ALICE opens her eyes, watches him for a while before speaking.

ALICE
Take the mirror.

YOUNG MAN

Hell an' damnation.

(Doesn't turn. He has a Cockney or Irish accent)

ALICE

The mirror is in the second drawer.

*(*YOUNG MAN *covers his ears)*

In the drawer. Should be.

(He turns)

YOUNG MAN

(Furious) What bloody mirror.

ALICE

Ah the voice of the real world. I knew it.

YOUNG MAN

(Staring at her) Yer mad. Right. Right.

ALICE

Is that the verdict in the dens from which you spring.

YOUNG MAN

They told me you was ill. That it'd be easy.

ALICE

Are you not very experienced. It sounds as if you're a
rank beginner.

YOUNG MAN

I don't believe this is bloody 'appening.

ALICE

A sentiment of which I partake almost daily.

YOUNG MAN
It ain't suppose to be like this.

ALICE
Don't be so conventional. Very few things are really impossible. What's your name.

YOUNG MAN
I said to one of me pals, you come along, I ain't sure about this job, it may be too big for me to go up alone, but he say, nah Tommy—

ALICE
Tommy.

YOUNG MAN
Why don't you scream.

ALICE
It appears that I'm not frightened.

YOUNG MAN

Scream for help, go on. This ain't a dream, right. Yer rich. You 'ave servants. Rich people can do anything they want. Why don't you scream.

ALICE
You don't frighten me.

(Off-stage noise of footsteps, voices. YOUNG MAN precipitously hides behind curtain of French doors—or under bed. ALICE slides down under covers, closes her eyes. Door opens: NURSE and HARRY enter. HARRY in evening dress—white tie, tails)

HARRY
(Whispering) I merely wanted to see how, see if, see that, see whether—

NURSE

70 She's been restless. She hardly ate today. Orange marmalade for breakfast.

HARRY

I don't want to wake her.

ALICE

(Tossing in the bed, her eyes still shut) Dejection. Innocence. Oh. The music. Harry.

HARRY

Just looking in dear heart.

ALICE

(Opens eyes) Where are you. I mean where were you.

HARRY

After the play—

NURSE

Wending his way home your ever-thoughtful—

ALICE

This is not the real world. I'm feeling quite large tonight. *(Laughs)* Quite broad-minded.

HARRY

I shall come tomorrow.

NURSE

I shall look in later.

*(*ALICE *sighs)*

You'll ring if you need me.

(They leave. YOUNG MAN *emerges from hiding)*

YOUNG MAN
Why did you do that. I mean, why didn't you tell 'em.

ALICE
You're sweating with fear.

YOUNG MAN
I'm not scared. It's hot under there. Sweet Jesus, my pals won't never believe this.

(Turns to go, then hesitates)

ALICE
I'd just offered you the mirror.

YOUNG MAN
(Turns back) Who was that.

ALICE
My brother.

YOUNG MAN
Thought it was yer father.

*(*ALICE *laughs)*

You ain't so old as I imagined.

ALICE
At what age did you take up burglary. Am I correct in supposing that there are not many women in your occupation.

YOUNG MAN
Women!

ALICE

7v Are there no women burglars.

YOUNG MAN

(Jeering) A woman cracksman. How could that be. That's
what I am. An' then there is a crow, that's always a bloke,
who keeps guard on the street, watchin' for a peeler or
someone who might notice. A canary, that's a woman
who carries the tools, if it's a big job, an' sometimes she
keeps watch on the street, like the crow does, but I don't
see a woman goin' up walls. That couldn't be. You don't
know nothin' about it.

ALICE

But why can't women climb walls, I could imagine a
woman climbing walls. In my country, in the West,
women carry guns and ride horses and perform feats of
daring quite unknown in this old-fashioned kingdom of
yours.

YOUNG MAN

Funny you talkin' about a woman climbin' walls, an' you
in bed all the time. You don't 'ave a 'usband, right.

(ALICE *shakes her head*)

Say, are you ailin' or are you, you know, cracked. It sure
sounded as you was ill.

ALICE

(As before, trance-like) Dejection. Innocence. Oh. The
music. What's your name.

YOUNG MAN

You mean you're pretendin', that's all. Really?

ALICE

No I'm really ill. I just like to make fun of myself. I can't
even get out of bed on my own.

(She gets up. YOUNG MAN *looks alarmed)*

Am I frightening you.

YOUNG MAN
You are cracked.

*(*ALICE *walks across room, turns on a light)*

If you call someone I'll have to stop you.

ALICE
But I'm not afraid of you. I can't help it. It's like that.

(She walks toward him)

YOUNG MAN
Don't you come near me.

ALICE
Don't be afraid of *me.* Why don't you do what you came to do.

YOUNG MAN
This ain't how it's suppose to be.

ALICE
I suppose it is very frightening.

YOUNG MAN
Out there on yer balcony 'fore I come in my heart hurt so much it was kickin' my chest, inside, kickin' hard, an' I felt dizzy an' my mouth was full of puke an' my pants full of piss an' then my foot touched the window an' I said, sh, sh, sh, to myself, easy Tommy-Tom, shhhhhh, an' then I took a swig, I brought a flask to keep up my spirits, an' I opened the door with my jemmy ever so soft

an' easy an' you was sleeping, you was snoring a little—

ALICE
Oh.

YOUNG MAN
Nah, it was nothin', you should hear how my ma snores.
An' then you spoiled everything an' woke up.

ALICE
What's in the flask.

YOUNG MAN
(Laughs) Gin, what else. Ya' think it was tea.

ALICE
May I have some.

YOUNG MAN
Sure, why not, why not, what else crazy thing do you
want.

(Produces flask from inside jacket, offers it to ALICE.
She takes it, drinks)

Give it back.

ALICE
In a minute. Does your mother call you Tommy-Tom.

YOUNG MAN
How do y' know that.

ALICE
Do you have many sisters and brothers.

(Drinks more)

YOUNG MAN

My ma birthed seventeen but some is dead. We're just
eleven left. I'm goin'. *(Pointing to flask)* Give it back now.

ALICE

And now you can't go through with it.

YOUNG MAN

I didn't come 'ere to talk. This is no talkin' job. 'Ere don't
drink it all.

ALICE

You're quitting. You can't do it now.

YOUNG MAN

I didn't say that. Yer putting words in my mouth. I didn't
say that.

ALICE

Am I stopping you. Is anything I'm doing stopping you.

*(He hesitates, glaring at her. For a moment it seems
as if he might strike* ALICE. *Then he turns away)*

Get on with it, young man.

(Muttering under his breath, YOUNG MAN *resumes his
burglary. He empties out a drawer with jewelry, puts
it in a carpetbag; takes shawls, figurines, a small
painting, puts them out on the balcony, pausing oc-
casionally to look at* ALICE—*who watches, leaning
against the piano, imperturbable, taking a swig now
and then from the flask)*

Surely you're not expecting me to pitch in and help.

*(*YOUNG MAN *hesitates)*

Take that, too.

76

(Points to vase of flowers)

YOUNG MAN
It ain't worth much.

ALICE
It is to me.

YOUNG MAN
D'ya 'ave any money.

ALICE
No money, no teaspoons.

YOUNG MAN
I didn't ask ya' for teaspoons. What's this.

(Holds up case)

ALICE
A gold pencil case.

YOUNG MAN
Imagine having gold for your pencils.

(Puts it in his bag)

Are you just goin' to stand there an' watch me.

ALICE
I've emptied your flask. It certainly has helped keep my
spirits up.

YOUNG MAN
Well I can't do this with you so close. Who do you think
I am.

(ALICE walks slowly back to bed)

Under the covers.

ALICE
I can't.

YOUNG MAN
You 'ave to.

ALICE
You don't seem to appreciate that I'm out of bed.

YOUNG MAN
Appreciate! Lord, is this somethin' to appreciate.

ALICE
I don't want to be in bed. You are an intruder. I can't be in bed with a stranger here.

YOUNG MAN
You 'ave to. Get in .

ALICE
You could take the bed. *(Laughs)* Take it,

YOUNG MAN
I don't want yer smelly bed. Get in the bed. Cracked!

ALICE
I'm sure I wouldn't want your bed either. I used to have a wooden bed, and curtains around it, but according to the newer theory, it is wood, even more than stale bedding and the enclosing curtains, that is to blame for the appearance of bedbugs. That is why I now have a brass bed.

YOUNG MAN

Only the rich don't 'ave bedbugs. Don't give me that about wood.

ALICE

I didn't mean all wooden beds. Bitter wood, imported from Jamaica, is believed to be unsavory to bugs.

YOUNG MAN

Get in bed.

ALICE

I'll walk up and down and ignore you.

(YOUNG MAN *looks again in one of the drawers, pulls the gilt mirror out, holds it up*)

If you take that I'll bless you.

YOUNG MAN

But it's nothin'. Wood!

(Puts sack and bag of tools on balcony)

ALICE

Sometimes I have such odd thoughts. My mind makes me feel strong. Makes me master. But I don't throw myself on anything. I just stay in my lair. Sometimes feeling—

YOUNG MAN

(Returning from balcony) At least sit down.

ALICE

No.

YOUNG MAN

I'm leavin'.

ALICE
I'm not very entertaining am I.

YOUNG MAN
That tall woman'll come back.

ALICE
No she won't.

YOUNG MAN
There's too much light.

(He turns down one of the two lamps)

ALICE
I see terrible thoughts when I close my eyes. But when I die I won't see them.

(YOUNG MAN, who has been packing up the loot, drops cut-glass Jubilee dish; it breaks)

Oh be careful.

YOUNG MAN
(Jeering, nervous) I thought ya' didn't care about your possessions. I thought you thought you was above all that . . .

ALICE
My detachment.

YOUNG MAN
Rich people!

ALICE
I see big things very small and small things so big. My father's leg. He's going to hurt me. This is a temple of tyrannical gentility.

YOUNG MAN
A what.

ALICE
There are so many terrible and engrossing things going
on in the world and I'm trapped inside this turbid self
that suffers, that closes me in, that makes me small.

YOUNG MAN
You wouldn't last one day where I come from.

ALICE
Out there, it is so big. I keep to my bed. But I ask Nurse
to leave the doors to the balcony open and from my bed
I hear. It reverberates within me. Once a whole family,
or what passes for a family, breaking apart, beneath my
window. In the stillness of the night the voice of a woman,
hardly human in its sound, saying without pause, in a
raucous monotone, "You're a loi-er. You're a loi-er" min-
gled with the drunken notes of a man and with a feeble
gin-suckled wail for chorus—

YOUNG MAN
Hardly human? Hardly human?

ALICE
Mentally no fate appalls me.

YOUNG MAN
Hardly human? An' what are you. You don't have to do
nothin' but lie here. What's so human about that.

ALICE
I express myself badly.

YOUNG MAN
I won't let you get at me anymore.

ALICE
I'm old enough to be your mother.

YOUNG MAN
Don't pull at me.

ALICE
I see we are not to be friends.

YOUNG MAN
Friends! Friends! At the Last Judgment I could be friends
with the likes o' you.

(Piercing whistle from outside. He closes carpetbag)

My signal. My crow. He must 'ave spotted someone.
(Gathers other gear)

You didn't see nothin'. I wasn't 'ere.

(Stoops; puts on shoes)

You could still send for the peelers an' tell 'em what I
look like an' they'd find me. You could do that. You do
whatever you want, don't you.

ALICE
What I do is mostly not do things. And so I shall. You
weren't here. (Laughs) And this isn't going to happen
again either. You won't find another mark as eagerly
posthumous, as mild, as curious as I.

(YOUNG MAN stands, hesitates)

YOUNG MAN
I'm sorry.

ALICE

82 Don't be sorry.

YOUNG MAN

I ain't an animal, you know. I'm a human being just like you.

ALICE

Now you are making me sad.

YOUNG MAN

I'm sorry yer not a well person an' I hope you get better, that's what I wanted to say.

(Whistle sound)

That's 'im, my pal.

ALICE

Crow.

(YOUNG MAN *opens French doors)*

I still think you could do something better with your time, your youth, with your horrid energies, with your—

(Doors slam shut: he is gone)

Out there it's so big.

(ALICE *walks to doors, draws curtains. Blackout)*

SCENE 8

ALICE's *bedroom. Stripped, except for bed, wheelchair in the corner, piano. Tall stack of mattresses in rear of stage, by curtainless doors to balcony.* ALICE *lying on top of the bed in street clothes (or covered with a paisley shawl).* NURSE *at the piano: scales. Sunset light.*

ALICE
I did get up.

NURSE
That's very important.

ALICE
Don't speak to me as if I were a child. You mean unimportant.

NURSE
Unimportant, I mean.

ALICE
Important—unimportant—unimportant—important.

NURSE
You did get up.

(NURSE *switches from scales to a fragment of the Parsifal theme, then back to scales*)

ALICE
Turning up the lights to get rid of those frightening shadows.

NURSE
You did get up.

ALICE
Even if I am grown up—

NURSE
Even if you don't get up again.

(NURSE *stands*)

ALICE
I should like to be a little larger. That doesn't seem much to ask. Stay with me.

NURSE
I will.

(NURSE *sits in wheelchair near bed*)

ALICE
You can read me a story, I'll tell you one.

NURSE
I will.

ALICE
Without the unhappy ending. We won't tell.

NURSE
I will.

ALICE

I used to be a real person or different. I tried. I feel as if
I fell.

NURSE

I'll catch you.

ALICE

Let me fall asleep. Let me wake up. Let me fall asleep.

NURSE

You will.

*(Room becomes brighter and brighter. Quick
blackout)*

CURTAIN

A NOTE

ON THE PLAY*

Suppose Shakespeare had a sister, a brilliant sister, a sister with a writing gift as immense as her brother's? That's what Virginia Woolf asks us to imagine in her epochal polemic *A Room of One's Own*. Is it likely that Judith Shakespeare—the name Woolf imagines for her—would have found the inner authority that could have made her a playwright? Or, as is more likely, would her gift have remained silent? Silent not merely for want of encouragement. Silent because of the way that women are defined and therefore, commonly, define themselves. For the obligation to be physically attractive and patient and nurturing and docile and sensitive and deferential to fathers (to brothers, to husbands) contradicts and *must* collide with the egocentricity and aggressiveness and the indifference to self that a large creative gift requires in order to flourish.

Shakespeare, as far as we know, did not have a sister. But the greatest American novelist, Henry James, whose brother was the greatest American psychologist and moral philosopher, William James, had a sister, a brilliant sister, and we know what she became. The waters of depression closed over her head when she was nineteen, she tried to summon the courage to commit suicide, she suffered from a variety of vague and debilitating ailments, she went abroad, she stayed in bed, she started a diary, she died . . . at forty-four.

So *Alice in Bed* is a play about women, about women's anguish and women's consciousness of self: a free fantasy based on a real person, Alice James, the youngest of five children (and only daughter) of an extraordinarily distinguished nineteenth-century American family. The father, heir to a large business fortune, was a well-known author on religious and moral subjects. An eccentric and strong-willed man, who had lost a leg in an accident at thirteen, he educated his children at home in Cambridge, Massachusetts, and took them on several trip to Europe when they were young. (Not surprisingly, the mother was a mild, retiring person who had little influence on the life of the family.) When Alice James had her first crisis, she is said to have made her desire to commit suicide known to her father, who, after a solemn lecture, granted his permission. In 1885 she moved to London, where her brother Henry ("Harry") had settled, and lived there, bedridden, until her death from breast cancer seven years later.

Perhaps nothing about a person is more potent, and also more arbitrary, than someone's name.

The name of my historical character, Alice James, inevitably echoes the nineteenth century's most famous Alice, the heroine of Lewis Carroll's *Alice in Wonderland*. The all too common reality of a woman who does not know what to do with her genius, her originality, her aggressiveness, and therefore becomes a career invalid, merged in my mind with the fictional figure of the Victorian girl-child who discovers the world of adult arbitrariness in the form of a dream (in the style produced by that perfectly legal and widely used nineteenth-century drug, opium) in which the changes in and perplexities about her feelings are imagined as arbitrary changes in physical size and scale.

And once Alice James, my Alice James, had fused with the Alice of *Alice in Wonderland*, I knew I could have a scene inspired by (though quite different from) the most famous chapter of Lewis Carroll's masterpiece, "A Mad Tea-party."

To my mad tea-party I have convened, for the purpose of advising and consoling Alice, the ghosts of two nineteenth-century American writers. One, Emily Dickinson, was a genius—who dealt with her searing originality by spending her life as a reclusive spinster, keeping house for her parents and brothers and sisters; of Dickinson's more than nine hundred poems, not one was published in her lifetime.

Margaret Fuller, the other writer summoned to the tea-party from beyond the grave, is the first important American woman of letters, who wrote a study of Goethe and a notorious proto-feminist book, *Woman in the Nineteenth Century*. She drowned with her young Italian husband and baby, when the ship bringing her back to America from Italy, where she had lived for some years, foundered in a storm a hundred feet or so off Fire Island, New York.

I have also convened to my tea-party two exemplary angry women from the nineteenth-century stage: Myrtha, the Queen of the Wilis, a company of ghosts of young women who, betrayed in love, have died before their wedding day, from Act II of *Giselle*; and from *Parsifal*, my Dormouse: Kundry, the bitter, guilt-ridden woman who wants to sleep.

After the crowded tea-party, a monologue. Alice, in her mind, must go to Rome—which her brother Harry often visited and where Margaret Fuller lived. And there she will imagine not only her freedom but the weight of the past and the distressing claims of the world beyond the privileged one in which she lives, represented by the figure of a child with a maimed hand.

A real encounter with a representative of the world that does not have the bourgeois luxury of psychological invalidism moves the play to its climax, when a young burglar enters the invalid's bedroom.

All is fiction, of course, in my play. Much is invented.

I wrote *Alice in Bed* in two weeks in January 1990, but I first dreamed it from beginning to end ten years earlier, in Rome, while rehearsing the production I directed of a late play by Pirandello, *As You Desire Me*—another play about a woman in despair who is, or is pretending to be, helpless.

I think I have been preparing to write *Alice in Bed* all my life.

A play, then, about the grief and anger of women; and, finally, a play about the imagination.

The reality of the mental prison. The triumphs of the imagination.

But the victories of the imagination are not enough.

90 *Written for the German translation of *Alice in Bed*, which had its premiere in Bonn, at the Municipal Theatre, in September 1991.